Emotional Intelligence

The Ultimate Beginner's Guide to Developing Control over Your Emotions, Build Self Confidence, Grow Great Relationships, and Find Long Lasting Success

Table of Contents

Introduction to Emotional Intelligence

"Emotions can get in the way or get you on the way." -- Mavis Mazhura

What it is and why you need more of it

EQ – this is the common abbreviation for 'Emotional Intelligence'. EQ is a personal skill, and not to be confused with IQ or your so-called Intelligence Quotient. EQ is "measured" in a much different way, as we will see in these pages. Although a case can be made that both IQ and EQ are subjective, most of us agree that IQ ends up as a *number* about someone's intelligence, whereas EQ ends up as an overall *feeling* and *connection* we have with an individual.

As EQ becomes better appreciated, large corporations are looking more frequently and openly for high EQ individuals, whatever their IQ! That is because people with strong EQs perform better – in terms of pure efficiency and effectiveness, and in human interactive terms.

So what is this thing we call EQ? To some degree, we all have EQ – some of us naturally have more than others. Any individual can consciously develop more of it. How we see the world, react to it, and behave in it with other people is *emotion-based*. In a nutshell, "having a high EQ" or "a good EQ" means that you are someone who understands what makes a human being tick, from an *emotional and reactive* standpoint. You are an individual who understands that we all see the world through eyeglasses clouded by feelings and emotions. You are able and willing, as a high EQ person, to adapt your own feelings and reactions to harmonize with those of others, or to position the situation for a better outcome for everyone involved.

Whew! Sounds complicated. But again, rest assured that we all have some degree of EQ – we are born with it! We are all natural observers; we can all position ourselves to create better outcomes in situations that might otherwise go sour. The catch is that we don't all have a full *awareness* of our EQ and how to use it effectively in all our interactions.

Emotional Intelligence has been much discussed, at least since the mid-1990s. It was a book by Daniel Goleman of the same name that started everyone buzzing about EQ.

Let's simplify a bit. Emotional Intelligence is, I believe, a three-part personal skill, and is much, much more than just "positive mindset".

- First of all, it is your non-judgmental recognition and awareness of your own emotions and feelings, and those of other individuals. It requires you only to pay attention – to observe.

- It is secondly your personal ability to control and express your own feelings in appropriate ways for the circumstances. And we all live in a variety of different circumstances. It requires some personal discipline.
- Thirdly, it is your ability to register what others' emotions may be as you interact with them, to acknowledge those feelings, and to self-manage your own emotions in order to create a harmonious exchange with those people. It requires your will to act according to facts and observation, not your emotions.

EQ is about Business

It was people in business who were the first ones to see the benefits of paying attention to their levels and usages of EQ. Emotional Intelligence is a personal skill set, and the most *effective, successful* and *respected* managers, leaders, business owners, sales people, politicians and influencers have a high degree of this skill. If salespeople were among the first professionals to realize that "personal development" was the best way to create more and easier business success (and a higher personal income because of more sales), others in business have imitated them – and improving their EQ is at the top of the personal development training that they do.

Business people indeed perked up when they heard about EQ. They are always looking for "an edge" – an edge over the competition, an edge in their internal effectiveness in people management, and an edge in time management. Their thinking is that every tiny bit of advantage expands exponentially into bigger end results. And they are right.

Developing more EQ for yourself is not reserved today only for business people, naturally. Any individual can train him- or herself into a higher level of EQ. Why you would do that is for the many benefits that you reap by doing so!

EQ is about Life

Would it be wise for all of us to recognize that we need more of this EQ quality? Undoubtedly! As the saying goes, what's good for the goose is good for the gander.

Getting along better with a worried spouse, a rebellious teenager, a sick grandparent, a difficult neighbor or a mean clerk at the store down the street ... that all becomes easier for people with a developed EQ.

In our life and living, we have relationships of many types. Relationships can be subject to misunderstandings, grumpiness, jealousy or envy and all sorts of other obstacles to simply getting along well. Connecting meaningfully with others and expressing your harmony and love together gets to be a challenge without high EQ. When we learn how to take feelings and emotions into account for ourselves as well as for the other person, and act from our new knowledge – relationships just flow more smoothly. Everyone is simply happier.

Perhaps you have already noticed – maybe in observing prominent individuals covered in the media – that the better the EQ, the better all relationships and personal interactions are too. Or maybe it is still pretty mysterious to you how to achieve this (don't worry – you'll get some guidance in the next few pages). There are countless benefits to being able to create more harmonious, smoother and more effective relationships – I think everyone would agree. Everyone on this planet has relationships with other individuals. Why not make them the happiest, most harmonious, and mutually satisfying that we can? _That_ is why EQ is so popular.

How to Use This Book:

Developing your EQ is experiential. That just means you have to do it to learn it. There are a

number of exercises in the following pages –
certainly not all the EQ exercises that teachers
have used over the years, but enough to get you
seriously on your way to a higher EQ. Do the
exercises.

Chapter 1 – No Denial Allowed in EQ

I can tell you this right now: You won't like all your feelings.

You can laugh as you read that, but it is time for a reality check about feelings. The fact is that all human beings have an oversupply of feelings. Males and females. Youngsters and elders. Rich and poor. First-world country dweller or Third-world resident. Leader or follower. We all have feelings. Lots and lots of them.

Not all of these feelings are pleasant to carry around. Some are downright ugly when they get out of control and interfere with any of our relationships – and this means the relationship you have with yourself as well as with others.

You might only be carrying around those awful feelings inside yourself – keeping them locked down tight, not expressing them outwardly. But that doesn't mean you're having a good time holding them inside. Keeping unwanted feelings under lock and key is hard work and takes a lot of energy!

Other times, those terrible feelings break loose and rip through your words and actions during a face-to-face exchange with someone – and then, well, everything seems to quickly deteriorate. Not fun.

If you are serious about developing a higher level of Emotional Intelligence, you can no longer be in denial about your anger problem or your insecurity issues, your panic attacks or your defensive reactions. These are all driven by emotions, and unpleasant ones at that! These types of issues interfere with your relationships with others; they may sabotage them entirely. These emotions insidiously interfere with your personal happiness and your sense of well-being out in the world.

If you are to "fix things", you have to acknowledge that you have these specific feelings. You have to acknowledge that they express themselves as behaviors, words and actions. Denial of this truth is not allowed!

That's the bad news. The good news is that you can do something about those unpleasant feelings. You cannot only do something about it – you can turn things around completely. You'll see how in the next pages. You can do something about the unpleasant ones (and an exuberance of the nicer ones, as appropriate) for one simple reason:

These are your feelings and you are the boss of them.

Pleasant or unpleasant feelings, wanted or unwanted? Whichever they are, you still have the ability to deal with them or even eliminate them. There are ways, as you will now see, to do so.

Self-Awareness First

So, no more denial. If you are on a path to developing more EQ for yourself, you must face this raw fact: Some of your feelings will be unpleasant or downright ugly to deal with. If you hate them, think about those who are "attacked" by them when you explode!
Your first step on the path to higher EQ is self-awareness. It about acknowledging what is. If you have out of control anger problems, that is "what is." Acknowledging this allows you to move into remedial actions.

EQ means you first work at understanding how *you* tick (or you can never hope to better understand others).

Let's just look at what self-awareness actually is.

When your physical body has a pain, you become aware of it pretty quickly. The pain is calling out for your attention; that is pain's function. When you notice it, you become aware. This awareness allows you to take appropriate healing actions. This is one form of *self*-awareness; no one else can feel what's going on in your physical body.

Another form of awareness is conscious information about the "type of individual" you are. Not all of us are clear about the type of personality or character that we operate from. For instance, we may be aware that we are a boisterous and loud life-of-the-party type of person, or a quiet wallflower who prefers to stay out of sight and operate only from behind the scenes. We may not be aware that people think we are tactless or abrasive! When you *accurately* identify your personality traits, you have self-awareness. From there, you can choose (or not) to take actions to change things.

The form of self-awareness we are speaking of in these pages is about the type of feelings that are stored inside you. Those feelings are probably visible to any attentive outside observer. For instance, others easily detect your shyness, your impatience, your disapproval, your sadness, your anger or frustration. Others are aware of these feelings within you. Now it is time for you to become fully *self*-aware of those feelings, and make a decision about them. The decision is this:

Are they beneficial to you in all of your relationships and interactions ... or not?

To develop greater self-awareness of the feelings that are already within you, follow the exercises below. A number of personal growth trainers use "emotions charts" of some form to help their trainees become more familiar with the vast range of feelings that humans deploy or store.

We all deploy some of our feelings, as a natural course of living. Most of those feelings are readily identifiable by us if we think a little bit about it. That means that we are conscious of them – they are part of our conscious mind and behaviors. We stuff down or store many other emotions in a sort of vault that psychologists call the subconscious mind.

EQ trainers will perhaps also help you recognize how some feelings are "heavier" than others. For instance, deep apathy or depression seem to literally pin us to the sofa, because they make us feel so heavy. We feel unwilling to take any action whatsoever. We cannot move. Other feelings are "lighter". These are feelings that energize us, such as joy, love, elation, and self-confidence. We are willing to jump up and do things when these feelings prevail.

Self-Awareness Exercises

Before I list exercises that help you develop your emotional self awareness, beware: Do not be deceived by their simplicity! Most people will not do this introspective, experiential work on themselves. They will blow it off as silly or ineffective. Don't make their mistake! Emotionally Intelligent individuals understand that feelings are really quite simple. Understanding feelings becomes easier – and very quickly, too – with these exercises.

Do the exercises every day. You may need to do them every day for several months – most people with even a developed EQ keep on high alert for feelings all the time. Aim for 7 straight days of practice, then add a week, then another. Don't get discouraged! Change is cumulative.

Keep a small notebook in your pocket or purse. You can buy them at any local store.

1. Find a premade list of human emotions. You may find one in a book and

photocopy it. You can Google "chart of emotions" or "list of feelings" or "inventory of feelings." Print it out. Fold the printout into your notebook.

You might come up with results like these, which I found on the first page of my search results today:

http://www.cnvc.org/sites/default/files/feelings_inventory_0.pdf
http://humanemotionschart.com/

Use the printout to regularly review and get familiar with all the feelings listed. Read each individual emotion and ask yourself the questions, "How do I express this feeling? When am I moved to express it?" Answer honestly!

Place a checkmark next to each feeling word you have examined in this way.

2. For this exercise, you will be observing and noting down the feelings that you personally _experience_ throughout the day and the circumstance.

   a. Use your notebook. No need to <u>do</u> anything about the feeling, just name it, and write it down. Keep a running list for the entire day. Your entry might look like this:

   > _May 3 –_
   > _Panic, late for work._
   > _Frustration, meeting with my assistant._
   > _Jealousy/envy, coworker got a compliment from the boss. Apathy, need to meet that deadline._

   b. After one week, and certainly after one month, of making these notes, review everything to date. Look for patterns. A pattern is any feeling that recurs – an emotion that you experience several or many times. You feel "exhilarated" 4 times, and in quite different circumstances each time. You feel "frustrated" 8 times, but notice that a single trigger set off 6 of those times. And so on. Patterns.

You will probably not experience a single and continuous emotional state from morning to night! No one does. You will notice patterns that create your emotional ebb and flow.

You will be able to discern a pattern, perhaps, about the type of feelings you have in the morning versus those of the afternoon or the evening. Remember what we said about the *heavy* energy versus *light* energy of our emotions.

You might try to find a pattern concerning your heavier emotions like sadness, indifference or fear. Do you mostly experience those late at night or in a 4 pm slump?

Likewise, try to find a pattern concerning your lighter emotions like enthusiasm or excitement, affection, self-confidence, so on. Is there a time of day that you are particularly light in this way?

Don't be disappointed if you don't find hard and fast patterns. Your goal is to develop awareness of your own emotions and how they flow for you from morning to night. Your goal is to identify the emotions that you experience throughout a day.

3. For this exercise, keep your notebook at your bedside. Your job is to identify and write down the _very first feeling_ you experience every morning. This is the very first one you have before rolling out of bed!

Again, after one week, and certainly after one month, you will notice patterns in your emotional state upon waking:

- Some people will notice that they are grumpy 8 mornings out of 10 as they roll out of bed.
- Others will roll out of bed 6 out of 10 days with a feeling of exuberance for the day to come.

In both cases, you now use that information to understand yourself better – to develop better self-awareness of your emotions, and when they *are likely* to occur. After all, if you can predict *when* they will pop up, you can take preventive action!

4. Each time you change activities in your day, write down the feeling you have about starting that new activity. Just write for instance:

Lunch appointment with prospect – feeling hungry, nervous.
Drive to client office – feeling excited, confident.

Remember that hunger, thirst, sleepiness, are feelings, too! We say, "I *feel* hungry, tired, thirsty, sleepy, drowsy" don't we?

Before EQ / After EQ

Jean had occasionally been accused of being grumpy to co-workers in the afternoons. So when she looked at her chart of emotions and began reviewing it to determine how she expressed every emotion, she got a surprise. She was only grumpy in the afternoons because she was so sleepy and hungry! She felt groggy and drowsy due to her hunger. Her "before" approach was to ignore and shove aside her sleepiness and her hunger – but it turned into grumpiness instead. This self-knowledge led her to eating a light but nourishing lunch every day instead of having a cup of coffee or soda. No more sleepiness. People stopped accusing her of being grumpy – because she was no longer compensating in that way.

Peter, on the other hand, shoved this exercise aside when he got to the word "anger". He was quite aware of his anger issue. So was his wife ... his boss ... and, he acknowledged with a lump of grief in his throat, so were his children. His anger made him interrupt the chart of emotions exercise! What he wanted to know was, firstly, what caused this anger and his outbursts when it overwhelmed him. The cause of his anger had always mystified him. Secondly, he just wanted to know how to get rid of it! His "after" story comes at the end of the next chapter, so read on.

Chapter 2 – No Feeling Is Eternal, or EQ Evolves

No destructive or unwanted feeling need sabotage you forever. You may sigh with relief. Letting go of feelings and emotions that do not serve your growth (or your relationships) is possible.

In spite of what might seem true at any given moment, feelings do indeed come and go. No feeling is really permanent. Do you want proof? Go to the park. Look at little children in the playground. One minute they're laughing hilariously together, and the next minute one or more of them is crying – but give them one more minute, and they're playing harmoniously again with the same little friends.

Be as little children – surely there a saying about that, because that is what Emotionally

Intelligent people do. They notice the feeling, let it go and move on. They imitate the children and let the unwanted feelings go right away. No dwelling on them. Let them go and return to your real job in life of having fun playing.

I'm sure there is a therapist somewhere who has measured how long the average feeling lasts. Feelings can be fleeting or seem to stick with us endlessly. You will soon see that there are easy ways to let go of virtually every feeling that you identify. You can release emotions, whether unpleasant and sabotaging in your relationships, or just annoying or limiting to you personally. You will see some easy exercises to do anywhere to achieve this.

The important part to understand is that *you have control.* You have a choice about what to do.

Choice #1: You could hang onto that negative or unpleasant feeling, mull it over, rehash it, bring it back out when you retell the story that "created" that feeling and go on and on about it. You could go on for years that way! It is commonly called "holding a grudge" or "being obsessed." In a very real sense, that is a conscious choice that you are making for yourself. However, that is not how to become Emotionally Intelligent!

Choice #2: A better, Emotionally Intelligent choice to make would be to learn how to identify and let go of that feeling – on the spot. See it. Let it go. Move on.

As your EQ grows, you subtly start to behave differently. In my experience, it will be other people noticing this about you before you do! You will perhaps have greater self-confidence (where before you were a shy wallflower, not daring to speak up). Or you will possibly be noticeably quieter/calmer in group settings (where before you were boisterous, or often interrupted everybody). Whatever your "before" personality, those around you will start noticing an "after" version of you. And it will be complimentary!

Dissipate like Clouds

To get a different perspective on how feelings are really fleeting or temporary, let's look at anger and decision-making. We are all pretty familiar with comments like "don't decide anything until you calm down." It is well known that it's hard to think straight when anger is controlling our every move and action. Indeed, many of us have heard angry individuals themselves state, "I can't think straight, I can't think straight." This definitely frustrates them!

The advice about not making any decisions until the anger has passed acknowledges that our mental capacity to analyze, sort through information and come to a weighted decision cannot occur when anger is clouding our mind. It also acknowledges that the anger feeling will pass. Anger is a cloud that passes, just like those clouds in the sky blow on through or dissipate.

It is not just this strong feeling we call anger that clouds our ability to think. Strong feelings of jealousy do the same. Feelings of panic and fear likewise lock up our brains. Burning feelings of lust and craving for something lock out thoughts of everything but the object of our lust, too.

To get along more happily in all the circumstances of our lives, it just makes sense to be able to identify those sabotaging mind-blocking feelings, and control them. Notice that I do not say, "manage" them. To many teachers dealing with emotional intelligence, managing a feeling or emotion simply means stuffing it down and ignoring it. You don't want to stuff it down – you want to eliminate it. Don't ignore it for one very good reason: It will come back to haunt you sometime in your future. Sooner or later, you'll have to deal with it. Why not now? You don't want it in your repertoire of feelings anymore. Not if it sabotages you in this awful way.

In the previous chapter, you practiced identifying different feelings as you experience them. You likewise looked at the charts of feelings, assuming that you have experienced each of them, and looked for how you have expressed them in the past. This all goes to awareness of your feelings. It comes from honest introspection.

Many of us have a routine way we express our feelings – these are the patterns you are starting to notice in yourself. Some teachers and therapists call these patterns "triggers", but it doesn't matter what you call them. It's important that you are aware of them in yourself.

Knowing that emotions are not permanent, that they are mobile or movable gives you power and control. Once you identify and become aware of those feelings, you can learn how to let them go. Once they are gone, they no longer sabotage you. And you have all your mental faculties back! In times of crisis, you no longer freeze up! In times of stress, you are totally present and in charge. When others need you, there you are, fully available. That is the goal – and those are some of the other benefits of strong Emotional Intelligence.

I have stated several times that you have control over your feelings. That control includes being able to let go of feelings _at will_.

Here is a two-fold way that the best mental health professionals teach their patients to let go of overwhelming feelings. It is very easy to do. You just have to remember to do it! You can do it anywhere, because _no one will see you do it_. Once you learn the two processes, all you need to do is practice it at the very moment a strong feeling arises within you.

Exercises

1. Mental Picture Release

Let's call the first exercise a Mental Picture Release. Where are the emotions in such an exercise? They are embedded in the picture! A majority of people see pictures in their mind's eye. (And if you don't, don't worry, the next exercise will help you out immensely.)

The problem with pictures on a mental movie screen is that most people just hang on to them, or return to them, or the pictures themselves seem to return unbidden. When the pictures represent memories that are unpleasant, sabotaging, or simply have you spinning in your mind so that you cannot focus on anything else – it's time to do this Mental Picture Release.

The feelings embedded in such pictures are responsible for pinning them in your mind. Those feelings are like glue. You can let that glue dissolve. You can let that glue called feelings go, right along with the picture.

First, because this is practice, call to mind a _situation with other people that did not go well for you personally_. Perhaps it was some discussion in a business meeting. Perhaps a conversation with a teenage child of yours that ended in yelling and doors slamming. Just remember a situation that did not go well for you.

Next, revisit that situation as picture(s) in your mind. See the expressions on the faces of other people. Remember their body language and visualize it. See where the event took place.

Now look at that situation and try to identify the one or two dominant emotions embedded in that story. It is those emotions that keep your mind returning to this picture of this situation that didn't go so well.

To release the whole thing – the visual pictures, as well as the feelings embedded in them – see the picture framed as if on a TV screen or a movie screen. You are the film projectionist, and you have a control panel that allows you to fade out the pictures on the screen. You have one dial on your console that does that for you. Turn the dial on the console to gradually fade out the picture on that movie screen of your mind. Fade the picture away a little more. Dissolve that picture a little more. Turn that dial down, and just tell the picture that you are fading it completely off the screen right now.

You are done when the screen of your mind is blank.

There are different versions of this release, which I list here. Choose one that works for you:

- Shine a spotlight on the screen, so that the images cannot be seen behind the brightness.
- Imagine a different button on your control panel that makes the image blurry. Keep making the image blurrier and blurrier until it's a gray, fuzzy mass that you just drop off the bottom of the screen.
- If your image is in color, imagine you have a dial on your control panel that drains the picture of its colors and turns it into black and white. It keeps on blending the black and white until they become gray. Then just let the gray mass drip off the bottom of your screen.
- Imagine your image is on a huge old-style black chalkboard. Just take an enormous eraser and erase the picture top to bottom and side to side until the chalkboard is blank.
- You are a fireman and the image in your mind is on fire! You point your pressure hose at the image until the whole "fire"

is doused, and you can't see any part of it anymore.

NOTE: It has been the experience of all practitioners of this Mental Picture Release that doing it once is never enough! Most people need to repeat the exercise six or eight more times before that specific mental picture no longer can form in their mind.

So how do you do that?

Just command your mind to give you that exact same picture again. Remember you are the boss of all of your feelings; you also have control over these mental pictures. Your mind must give you the picture if it is still stored somewhere inside you. *The mind will attempt to re-create the exact same picture for you.* Please be aware that, as you do the releasement of the picture and its embedded feelings, the picture itself will morph, shift, and change. That is, parts of it have been let go, but not all of it. Take what you get on that movie screen of your mind, and release what you see.

You just call the picture up again and do the letting go or releasement of it until the screen is blank. You call the picture up one more time, do the releasement until the screen is blank. And again and again – as many times as needed until the mind is incapable of giving you that picture and your mental screen remains blank.

The natural conclusion of this release is when your mental screen remains blank (when your mind can no longer give you that specific image), you are completely free of that picture and all the feelings embedded in it.

2. Body-Based Feeling Release
The second simple exercise for letting go of feelings is not focused mentally, but in your physical body. When you become aware of feelings that have collected somewhere in your

body, this is the exercise you use to permanently let them go.

Right now, think of a situation in your life that _worries_ you. (It doesn't matter if you see a mental image or not for this releasement exercise.) Just think of something that worries you. It could be in relation to another person, or a circumstance in your life.

As you hold this worrisome circumstance in mind, bring your internal awareness to your physical body. Do you notice any tightness, grabbing or cramping anywhere in your throat, or your chest, or maybe your solar plexus or abs? Take a moment right now to notice this before you read on. Find the place in your body that has this new tightness or cramping.

When you have located this tightness in your body – congratulations! That tightness or cramping feeling that collected in your throat, or your chest somewhere, or in your gut, _is your feeling of worry._

The beauty of doing this type of release of feelings is that we are so very aware of what's going on in our bodies. We have a very intimate relationship with our body, if you think about it. We know it's every quirk, discomfort and pain. That is how it is so easy to locate our feelings. That is how, as you will now see, it is so easy to let them go.

Here is how to let go of this feeling that you have noticed in your body, in the specific collection of tightness or cramping in one part of your body.

Think again right now about that thing that worries you. Just to familiarize yourself with the process, place one hand over the area of your body where the feeling has collected as a tightness or cramping. This means you will put your hand over your throat, on your chest or over your gut. (Really, it could be anywhere on your body. Some people experience it behind the eyes or in the jaw. Just notice and put your hand over the cramping area.) This will focus your inner attention.

Now, in your mind's eye, imagine a *door or a window* over that cramping. *Open* the door or window. Mentally invite that cramping feeling – in this case, your *worry* feeling – to escape or float out the opening you have made. Just allow it to leave. Just assume that it does leave. And in your mind's eye? *Watch* it leave! Keep on telling it to leave, until you feel no more cramping, pressure or tightness in that area of the body. That is how you know you have completed the release of the feeling.

Remember that you are in charge. You have total control over your feelings and they must do as you say. Even "inviting" them to leave through the opening is a command to them. They must obey it. So watch the feeling leave out of that door until you don't feel any more cramping or tightness in that part of your body. That's it.

This process may take 30 seconds or three minutes. It depends how focused you are. It depends how strong the feeling actually is when you begin. But remember that you are the boss of your feelings, and they must do as you tell them to. Making the opening over the cramping area just facilitates them all paying your orders.

Seriously Simple

The beauty of the Mental Picture Release and the Body-Based Release is this: They are simple, discreet (no one sees you doing them)

and effective ways to get totally free of
unwanted feelings. The former takes away the
recurring visualization of unpleasant
circumstances as well as all of the feelings
embedded within it; the latter acknowledges
the feeling and removes it on the spot.

U.S. Veterans' Hospital mental health
professionals sometimes teach this process to
military returning from active war zones. It is
just one part of some PTSD treatments.
Needless to say, it is very effective. More than
one war veteran has said about both of the
exercises in this chapter that they have allowed
them to "stop looking over their shoulder." No
small compliment for such an easy pair of
exercises!

If that is not validation enough, monks and
nuns in Buddhist temples and Indian ashrams
have been doing this pair of releasement
exercises literally for centuries to great effect.
They develop self-awareness, certainly – but
also create a quiet, peaceful mind and body

which are free of unwanted feelings and mental pictures.

Before EQ / After EQ

Let's go back to check on Peter, from the previous chapter, who had no difficulty identifying his feelings of anger. In this chapter and its exercises, he was still a bit frustrated that there was no explanation to help him find the cause of his anger. (He realized in the end that he never needed to know how, when and where it started!) He went ahead and did the Body-Based Release of his anger. His anger always built up to explosion level within 10 minutes of waking up every day, so that is when he began to do the release exercises – first thing upon waking, when he felt the anger start to rise up. Then anytime during the morning when the feeling threatened, he did the exercises again. Afternoon, evening, before bed – he was relentless. He did it over and over again, anytime the anger reared its ugly head. After 10 days of doing the Body-Based exercise with his feeling of anger, something interesting happened. After breakfast one morning, his wife broke down in tears. Long story short, the day before, Peter had had no instances of anger – not verbal, not physical – with her or the children. None. For 3 mornings in a row, including this morning, Peter had not displayed any of the usual buildup to anger as before. She was actually crying in relief and hope! It was then that he revealed the exercises he had been doing.

Craig was a Vietnam veteran. His body came back whole and sound, but as he said, "my mind, not so much." Decades later, he was still carrying pictures of his devastating experiences around with him in his head. What interested him about the Mental Picture Release was that he could also let go of the body-based feelings that came up every time he saw the pictures. Those feelings were a bundle of fear, stress, shame, anger, grief and more. Once he learned both releases, he applied them both to his mental war pictures. He consciously sat three or four times each day after learning these releases, and told his mind to bring up the pictures. He would just sit and do the releases for 15 or 30 minutes – whatever it took. About two weeks later, his comments included this, "I've got my life back." When the pictures came up, he knew what to do. When he got the cramping or clutching in his chest or throat, he knew what to do. Soon, all of those devastating emotional war pictures in his head were gone, along with the body-based feelings they stirred up.

Chapter 3 – Personal Responsibility for Your EQ

"75% of careers are derailed for reasons related to emotional competencies, including inability to handle interpersonal problems; unsatisfactory team leadership during times of difficulty or conflict; or inability to adapt to change or elicit trust." -- The Center for Creative Leadership

The best self-growth trainers and teachers know at least one method for "releasement of unwanted emotions". You now know two methods for dealing with feelings. Teachers call it by different names: releasement, releasing, letting go, dumping, trashing, kicking out, cutting loose, tapping it out, setting it free, and on and on. These teachers understand the importance of positive EQ ... and that we are just better off when those undesirable feelings are permanently gone!

Remember that you are the boss of your feelings, whether that feeling is exuberant ecstasy or deep depression. What very few people realize, even those who have done a great deal of personal growth training, is that your feelings are at your command, quite literally. When you command a feeling to let you go, in other words – it must go. Sounds easy, so what's the rub with that? We get lazy about taking charge of our feelings!

You have to do change work yourself. No denial. No waiting till tomorrow, when it was this morning that you had that blowout with your spouse.

All of these experiential exercises can be done on the spot, and no one will be the wiser that you are doing it. If smokers leave the room or the building to take a smoking break, you also can take a feeling-releasement break. If those who drink a gallon of water at their desks every day need to take a break to go to the restroom periodically, you also can take a rest to do some releasing of those unwanted feelings.

It is your personal responsibility to make room for that break in your day. It's all about how badly you want to fix things. No one can let go in your place of that feeling of frustration you had during your business meeting. Take the time and let it go.

You may certainly have a high degree of skill in a specific technical job or professional arena. That says very little about what your EQ may be. I think you get the point that you are responsible for training up and developing your own EQ, regardless of training classes that you may attend. "In one ear and out the other" sorts of training seminars do nothing to develop your EQ. They do nothing to develop your awareness of self, of your feelings, of your behaviors and reactivities. They do nothing to help you make needed change. You have to put in the time yourself.

As stated by the Center for Creative Leadership in the quote at the beginning of the chapter, far too many people lose their jobs – or simply don't get ahead in a chosen career – because of their lack of EQ. What is more, a large proportion of those individuals remain in denial (or ignorance, which nowadays should not be a permitted excuse) about their low EQ. The information is now out there in abundance, so denial that there is any problem, or excuses that you don't know how to train up, just don't cut it anymore! You have to take responsibility for this aspect not only of your workforce skills, but for your ability to be effective in interpersonal situations of all kinds (both professional and personal).

Be Your Own EQ Doctor

As we saw with Peter and his experience with anger, humans with uncontrolled emotions can be quite dangerous to each other! When we do not take responsibility – or we are not aware that we even have personal control – we are a threatening being. Without control over our feelings, the behaviors they drive, our thinking and our mental pictures, we can be a danger to ourselves and to others. And there is no reason for it!

What I have not yet mentioned in these pages is that it is not only the unwanted or unpleasant feelings which you can do with the exercises on developing your EQ. Any persistent feeling or behavior, negative or not, qualifies.

- Perhaps you are overly courageous to the point of recklessness. A sort of extreme-sport spontaneity, where you leap before you think. Courage is ordinarily a lighter feeling, but it plays against you. Do the exercises to let go of your reckless courage feelings! Do the exercises to let go of mental pictures that the feelings stir up for you.
- Maybe you have lust for things that you have not identified as harmful to you.

Do the releasing exercises for the feeling of lust just to see what happens.

- o Craving and lust may not seem like "dangerous" feelings, unless they destroy your health by leading you to overeating.
- o Craving and lust to spend may not seem dangerous, unless they destroy your finances and put you and your loved ones in the street, from your overspending or bankruptcy!

- You might be the one that interrupts all speakers and all conversations to speak your piece, or to be humorous. Not dangerous, you say? Maybe it is to your career! Release the lust to interrupt and see what happens.

In other words, be aware of what your ordinary mind will judge as unpleasant or not. Sometimes you will discover that your noisy mind works against you and against your best interests. You will start to see how the mind is not always your ally.

This said, you will discover as you let go of the strongly unpleasant feelings and come into some control of them, that your quiet, peaceful and otherwise positive and loving feelings are starting to shine forth all on their own. When this happens for people, they are a bit surprised. They are under the impression that they need to reprogram themselves somehow for the positive, loving feelings. Not so! They were there all along, underneath the negative, unpleasant feelings and pictures.

This is why most EQ exercises focus on the unpleasant feelings. Once those unpleasant, destructive or sabotaging feelings and mental pictures are gone, the behaviors that were formerly driven by them can no longer materialize. What does materialize is an ability to think better, reason and analyze more clearly. You start to use your natural creativity to solve problems or to manage crises and dramas that other people or circumstances bring to you. You start to feel a greater self-possession, self-confidence and a better "big picture" view of circumstances. You always had this quiet ability – it was just hidden under sabotaging, heavy or unpleasant feelings and pictures.

You must take personal responsibility for the feelings you have – and for your reactions and behaviors that are triggered by them. It is 100% possible to choose the feelings that you express. You have exercises below on how to achieve that.

Attitude and Perspective

How you feel is a decision that you make. How you express any of your feelings is likewise a personal decision. Decision-making is within your control – and you have more and more control as your EQ levels grow. When you develop your EQ ability to consciously decide which feeling you will express, you are able to not only manage feelings that spontaneously arise (and that may be sabotaging to you), but you can shift from one feeling to another at will. It is a matter of shifting your attitude and perspective.

Exercises

1. Opposites Exercise

This is an awareness exercise to assist you in making a shift in your *attitude* and *perspective*. This is a good skill to have in times when your knee-jerk feelings are trying to control the circumstances.

- Do this when you are alone. Go back to your printout or master chart of feelings. Quietly, slowly read aloud each word on the chart.
- As you read, pause and bring your inner attention to your physical body. Notice which word(s) brings a physical cramping or clutching in your throat,

chest or gut. Do the Body-Based Release until the tightness is gone.

- What is the antonym or opposite of that feeling word? For instance, the opposite of Fear is Courage; the antonym of Sad is Happy. As you state the opposite feeling word to yourself, do you also get that clutching in your throat, chest or gut? If yes, do the Body-Based Release until the tightness is gone. Then go to the next feeling word on the list and repeat this process.

Do this for every word that you read that gives you a cramping or tightness in your body. Make a separate list of the feeling words you reacted to. Also note the antonym or opposite feeling word next to it.

2. Shifting

This exercise is a continuation of the prior one
– you will need your list of opposite feeling
words.

Let's say you reacted to Fear, whose
antonym is Courage. Your job in this
exercise is to _consciously_ _choose_ courage
– decide to experience courageousness
in your body!

The emotions you feel are a personal
decision. You are responsible for each of
your decisions. You can choose which
decisions to act on or not, wouldn't you
agree?

In your mind's and your body's memory,
decide to feel Fear right now.
Remember a situation that stirred up
some fear in you. Feel the cramping
tightness in your throat, chest or
tummy? Just make the decision to feel
it and what your body does.

Now make the opposite decision –
decide to experience Courage in your
body. You might throw your shoulders
back and lift your chin. Sit or stand
straighter and taller. You might
remember a time when you acted from
courage (as opposed to reacting from
fear or panic). Decide to feel courage in
your body.

Go back and forth between Fear and
Courage several times. Do this until you
experience each feeling palpably in your
body *on demand*. Notice how your body
shifts its positions. Notice how your
body feels differently with each opposite
feeling.

Now do the same back and forth
exercise with a different pair of feelings
from your list. Or try the exercise again
with any of these pairs:

• Sadness/Happiness

- Nervousness/Calm
- Outrage/Acceptance

Do you see how you can choose to feel sad, or choose to feel happy? It is totally within your control. Keep practicing! Choose all the heavy feelings that you find recurring in yourself, identify their opposites – and choose to experience their lighter, more positive opposite more frequently.

Practice this in real-life situations. Just pause as you take in the circumstances, and consciously shift from say, "aggravation" to "acceptance" and so on. Don't react from the initial feeling. Act from the new perspective. In fact, you might discover that all you need to do is to "choose to act from calm." It helps you think more clearly, speak and act with greater understanding and compassion.

Before EQ / After EQ

Marion tested with a high IQ, but her low EQ was holding her back in her career. She'd landed a satisfying, well-paid job in her competitive profession. However, she was always passed over when it came time for others to listen to her ideas in brainstorming sessions with colleagues – and she would never put her foot down and demand to have her say. Also, when any client said "No!" she was at a loss to come up with ideas to turn him around ... until two hours later in the quiet of her office. Lost opportunities ...

A comment by a close friend led her to studying and developing her own EQ. She did the very exercises in this book. Some emotions that she discovered in herself were quite a shock, but she worked hard on them. She did the letting go and shifting perspective exercises relentlessly. She developed more courage and confidence by *choosing* those feelings.

Finally, one day in yet another brainstorming session, she simply raised her hand, stood up with resolve, and started speaking with a strong, confident voice. For a few seconds one or two colleagues spoke over her. Then they were shushed by the boss. Marion's ideas were met with enthusiasm by all. She was off and running in a whole new direction, fueled by her higher EQ.

Chapter 4 – Improve All Your Interactions with EQ

"Knowing others and knowing oneself, in one hundred battles no danger. Not knowing the other and knowing oneself, one victory for one loss. Not knowing the other and not knowing oneself, in every battle certain defeat." -- Sun Tzu, *The Art of War*

Human interactions are smooth or bumpy based on your interpersonal skills. If, in your workplace job, you always feel like you're putting out fires started by rocky relationships, misunderstandings and rough interactions amongst various coworkers, then you'd better look to EQ training as a better solution. Gain back the time that you used to spend dealing with interpersonal drama to do real, productive, profit-generating work!

It is extraordinarily helpful to have entire groups of people in the workplace learn how to develop their own EQ in a formalized way. Before you get your company to take that step, though, there is more you can do on your own. Make your own life easier by developing *your* awareness of *other people's* emotions, reactions, behaviors, and adapt your own to them. Because you are now emotionally more self-aware, you are *more* emotionally *flexible* than before. Use that newfound flexibility to "be the bigger person" so to speak. Adapt to others' needs by bending your own just a bit.

If this sounds a little drastic, it really isn't! Rest assured it is about awareness plus flexibility. This is definitely within your reach.

When you make a big deal of applying your high Emotional Intelligence in home and work settings, life is fun, loving, creative and harmonious. Even the American National Institutes of Health have long been interested in EQ and studied the relationship (among others) between high/low emotional intelligence and ... successful marriages!

Marriage partner, business partner, family member, staff member – we are just speaking of relationships! They are fraught with feelings and the behaviors driven by them.

As you have developed awareness of your own feelings, reactions and behaviors, your EQ has necessarily improved. Now it is time to observe how other peoples' emotions and feelings lead them to act and react as they do. All you are doing is using your understanding of emotions and how they drive behavior to predict or estimate how others will act in workplace or home life situations.

You have now had practice identifying, acknowledging and somewhat controlling your own emotions prior to speaking or acting. It should now be a bit easier to guess where other people are coming from, in terms of emotions, reactivity and behaviors. They are just like you, in that they operate based on feelings!

Adapt, Don't Judge

With very little observation, you might immediately see an individual's dominant emotions. You might even notice a pattern of behavior in that person. Make no comment – perhaps that individual does not realize he has those traits! Don't be surprised that he has not developed self-awareness. Since your own EQ is rising, it is your job to make the greater effort in social interactions with this type of individual.

This is not about judging others in any way. Make no mistake – you must be a neutral observer, making no comment or judgment for or against that person. You are using the knowledge you have just gained about the individual to understand how you yourself now need to adapt to get along in this conversation or interaction with him.

Your knowledge of emotions and how they drive our behaviors is about learning, through observation, what makes others tick. This gives you an edge in *successfully* communicating and interacting with them. You have some exercises and tips in this chapter to help you improve your observation powers.

Exercises

Alongside information about taking personal responsibility for your feelings, words and behaviors, do what many high-EQ parents do: Teach your kids how to do some of this work. It is guaranteed to make their own relationships happier – in the home, in school and out in the world. By the way, some progressive schools are beginning to teach EQ tools in the classroom.

1. This exercise is about helping your children understand that feelings are natural, but that they also have control

over them. Help your children monitor and control their feelings and make better choices.

When you see your child expressing some feeling, even though it is clear which feeling to you, stop! Don't act or react in your pre-EQ way! Pause and find out from your child what's going on first. Ask your child, "Are you a little frustrated right now, or is something else going on?" Or, among the lighter feelings you notice, you may ask, "It seems like you're feeling very happy – is that true?" And then just listen.

That's the first step with this exercise. It brings to your child's attention that you have good "feeling awareness." You are no longer acting like the "bossy dad" or "rushed mom." It shows that you are concerned about your child's well-being.

Step two of this exercise is to tell your child outright that you are learning how to let go of your own unwanted feelings. Just do a Mental Picture or a Body-Based release, and ask your child if he noticed you doing anything. Of course, he won't see you doing anything! And that's the point you are making with the child. He too can do this exercise anywhere when he needs to.

Step three is to sit down when your child feels overwhelmed with some emotion or another from an unpleasant circumstance and just walk him through the Body-Based Release. Anyone can do it, as you know – demonstrate to your child that he can too.

Show that you are someone who can support others – find out what they need and give it to them when possible; create environments for them to thrive; develop their strengths.

2. A workplace exercise that you can do – whether you are a supervisor, owner, or an employee on a team – is the one that might have helped Marion. But she obviously did not have a manager expressing a strong EQ, did she? Be that high EQ manager for the Marion-types of your workplace!

Without me telling you how to do it, sit down with pen and paper and brainstorm how you would assist someone like Marion to express herself more confidently in those group settings.

Remember that you do not want to trample other people's feelings, either! So, for instance, you would never just tell the other members of the group to shut up. That is not a high EQ approach.

Before EQ / After EQ

Sean and his wife learned some of these exercises in a workplace seminar. Their youngest son, aged six, was being bullied in school. It was a hard kindergarten year for him! Having developed their own awareness and EQ, they sensed their son was troubled and coaxed out the reason. Every evening at bedtime, Sean sat with his son and did a Body-Based Release of his son's feelings about the matter. The child identified "fear" as the dominant feeling. They did this "letting go" quietly together every evening. The child saw the fear as "black icky smoke" pouring out of the opening he'd made in his chest. By the end of the second week, Sean was told by his son, "Dad, I don't have any fear left. Could you tell me a bedtime story instead?" Even children can develop greater EQ!

Chapter 5 – EQ, Business and Leadership

EQ has been a buzzword for many years now in the world of business. There is an excellent reason for that. Salespeople were probably the earliest adopters. Salespeople with a highly developed EQ sell more goods and services – and get more repeat business. So naturally others in the world of business want some of that edge, too!

Business

All of us in any "people business" reap great benefit from developing our EQ. When the boss has solid EQ, and has trained all staff in developing their own, lots of things shift for the good. Here are some ways EQ makes work life easier, not to mention more fun, more profitable, less stressful and tiring ...

- Business people of all professions and positions who have a high EQ have more extensive and productive networks – and more help flows in when they need it.
- Dealing with any high EQ individual in the workplace is always more relaxing, friendly, and harmonious.
- Resolution of conflict amongst individuals (staff or outsiders) with developed EQ is quiet and quick.
- Customers sense that things in your company are harmonious, honest and happy – and prefer doing business and repeat/referral business with you. They *feel good* when dealing with you!

If all this sounds like a world of work that you would prefer to evolve in every day, EQ is something you need to develop, use ... and offer as training to all of your employees.

Nobody likes to work for a manager or boss who can't control his temper, his moods or his words. A well-known statistic in the world of human resource management is that the majority of individuals leaving any job do so to get away from a poor supervisor or manager. In other words – a poor leader, with little to no EQ!

Leadership

A leader is simply any individual possessing a number of qualities that persuade others to follow them. Not every executive in corporations is a leader. Not every supervisor managing dozens of individuals in a department is a leader, either! Leadership is not a job title; it is a set of personality traits and behaviors.

As I've mentioned elsewhere, corporations and businesses are now looking for more people with high EQ because those individuals tend to be natural leaders. They get more done, have a better bottom line result year after year, and less staff turnover on their teams.

What defines a leader? A person with a developed Emotional Intelligence, of course! Here is why:

- High EQ pushes you quite naturally to listening more actively and attentively to other individuals. This is a good way to collect more information and data, which in turn helps decision-making.
- A developed EQ pushes you quite naturally to helping other individuals thrive, grow and express themselves. People working for/with you love you for this!
- A strong EQ individual does not *react*, but assesses the emotional and factual data before him so that he can *act* in an effective manner. That makes this emotionally savvy individual very adaptable to a variety of circumstances and personalities.
- A high EQ individual in a management role understands what it takes to develop teams and to assign work to

individuals in it – so that everyone thrives and contributes from their strengths.

- A high EQ manager will not only be a role model to his people, but *invest* in them in all senses of that term.
- An individual working on his EQ knows when it is time to regroup and when it is time to take a risk.
- A high EQ person is very likely to be goal-oriented for himself, and to understand how to help others set goals that are satisfying and achievable.

Defining a high EQ individual is essentially defining a leader. This is why more and more businesses and corporations want to hire more and more high EQ staff, managers and executives.

Exercises

1. Reaction or Action?

We have said it before in these pages, but now it is time to focus your budding EQ skills on reaction versus action.

In this exercise to build your awareness, you will be watching how other individuals either react from knee-jerk emotional push – or act after pausing and reflecting.

When you are out shopping, watch how:

- parents interact with their children
- teens interact with each other
- adult couples, or pairs of friends, interact with each other
- sales personnel interact, or fail to, with customers
- customers feel about sales personnel

Make mental notes about your observations. What are your personal judgments or feelings about what you are seeing? Make note of those and if you need to do a Body-Based Release as you observe, do so.

2. The second exercise is quite similar. You will choose a professional/business event or meeting as the setting for this one. Choose an event in which you do not need to participate very much.

Watch how:

- The official leader directs proceedings. Why is the person good or poor at it?
- Is there an unofficial, self-appointed leader, and how do you know?
- The leader goes about obtaining full participation, or failing to.
- Participants act during the meeting (bored, frustrated, impatient, spaced out, etc.)

As an individual with developed EQ, how would you conduct this same meeting? As a high EQ person, how would you participate in such a meeting or event? Don't make anyone wrong. That's not the exercise. Observe how others operate, and what you would do differently in their shoes, if anything. What would you imitate?

Before EQ / After EQ

Cameron was a staff member of a marketing team in a medium-sized company. She was quite frustrated by one person's domination of all of their creative meetings. She was frustrated that even the team leader caved in and let this other individual dominate. No one else got to express their creative opinions on anything! She had heard about and worked a bit on her EQ, and how to build self-confidence, and thought she'd give her new knowledge a try at the next meeting.

The team leader opened the meeting, and the overbearing individual interrupted and started stating his case. Cameron gently raised her hand, immediately stood up and addressed the team leader specifically, by looking him straight in the eyes. She said something like this, "I understand that Joe has many good ideas. But you are forgetting that there are six other people in the room and we have many good ideas as well. I would love to give you two ideas for last week's topic and three ideas for this morning's topic – if Joe would give me the floor for six minutes. Do you agree, boss?" She then jumped right in to her ideas! In a sense, she put her boss on the spot. Maybe that's what was needed, because every time Joe tried to intervene, the boss waved him quiet. On the strength of Cameron's courage, two other people during that same meeting made good contributions that were noted by all. Cameron shifted the *perspective* of the entire team at that meeting. Joe got a word or two in, and didn't feel left out.

Cameron's boss had an "EQ lightbulb" go off for himself that day. He realized that he had been a nonchalant, hands-off boss and that it obviously wasn't working! From that day forward, he made sure that everyone had the floor in those meetings, and he listened actively when anyone spoke. After 4 months of gentle, conscious shifting of his people-management style, his team's results shifted for the better, too. And after a year, top brass wanted to know his secrets for getting such great team performance. Cameron was not, by far, the sole beneficiary of her daring that day in the meeting!

"A growing number of organizations are now convinced that people's ability to understand and to manage their emotions improves their performance, their collaboration with colleagues, and their interaction with customers." FastCompany

Conclusion

"Emotional intelligence is the ability to sense, understand, and effectively apply the power and acumen of emotions as a source of human energy, information, connection, and influence." -- Robert K. Cooper, Ph.D.

Life is a fabulous roller-coaster ride during which we cannot always choose what happens to us. We can, however, choose how we react to it. We can be aware of the role feelings can play. We have direct control of our feelings, our attitude and our perspective on events of life and living. We can help others be in better control, too.

You can read Daniel Goleman's 1995 book, *'Emotional Intelligence'*, but these five points sum up what Emotional Intelligence is, according to him:

1. Self-Awareness
2. Self-Regulation
3. Self- or Internal Motivation
4. Empathy
5. Social Skills

We looked at emotional self-awareness in the first chapter. We examined how to develop more of it. Jean acquired new awareness about herself and made beneficial changes. Peter, on the other hand, was ready to let go of a destructive feeling he had long been aware of – his need was for an effective method to do so.

Self-regulation is all about controlling your body's behaviors and the words coming out of your mouth through conscious decisions. It is about biting your tongue and examining your feelings, and those of people you are interacting with, before speaking. In a leadership role, it is about positioning your approach before speaking or acting; you position yourself in relation to your observations of others and their needs. Craig was relieved to get his life back – to take back control – from fearsome mental pictures and the damaging feelings they contained.

Self-motivation can be multifaceted. For our purposes, it's really two things. First, it is understanding why you're involved in this particular interaction and what you wish to gain or achieve from it. It is also about determining if the others agree with you! Second, it is about being a life-long, self-motivated learner, someone who is teachable. Be someone willing to throw out old or false information and take in what's new and true. Marion took her personal power back by learning what was necessary to be more effective in her chosen professional roles.

Empathy is connection, and it comes into play when you pause for a moment of self-regulation and analysis of the situation. You will not flail your arms around and shout with an excited voice when you are interacting with a shy wallflower. That is not conducive to a good connection with that individual! You allow yourself to see the circumstances through the other person's eyes. Only then do you make your decision. Cameron's boss, who had lost his connection with his team, took charge of himself, developed more empathy and connectivity. His management style shifted to everyone's benefit.

Social skills are simply all about effective communication. When someone says that "Mister Brown has no social skills", what they really mean is he has a low (or no) EQ! Leaders excel at social skills, particularly conflict resolution, ability to critique and praise others effectively, remember important information about people, and so on. Sean's son got more comfortable around those who bullied him, by learning that feelings are not forever.

Do the exercises in these pages; be watchful; bite your tongue. This is all a great start at developing more Emotional Intelligence.

Remember that EQ is quite different from IQ. Getting along in a workplace environment is not about IQ, so much as your application of EQ. Developing more EQ for yourself is a question of personal study, observation and attention. Again, do the experiential exercises. Make up others that serve your needs. Go to EQ seminar training. Be watchful of your reactivity to other people's comments and behaviors – and bite your tongue before you speak. That will give you a few seconds to reflect on the emotions and feelings at play in this current interaction.

Not all highly Emotionally Intelligent individuals have a leadership job title or a large sphere of influence. But they are the ones people prefer to follow! All our most revered leaders have high EQs, if you examine their personalities and behaviors closely. Be that leader!

BEFORE YOU GO

If you liked this book you may like these other books from Mark Thomas

Check out more books by Mark Thomas

Free Bonus

As Promised Here Is Your Guide To
Creating More Hours In Your Day:
Discover How To Fit 48 Hours Of Work
In A Day

GET YOUR FREE COPY

LEARN HOW TO GET MORE DONE IN A DAY

Do you feel stuck, stressed, and pissed because you aren't able to get all of your most important tasks done in a day? Perhaps this book can be the answer to your struggles. Learn the ways to manage your time to get more things done in a day and free up time do things you enjoy in life. Procrastination and Distractions are the biggest enemy of time management. This book will teach you the exact strategies to conquer procrastination.

Download "The Clockwork Course" For FREE

If You Want Free Best Selling Kindle Books Delivered Straight To Your Inbox

JOIN OUR FREE KINDLE BOOK CLUB!

BE PART OF THE CLUB

Chapter One – The Money Mindset

Before you even begin to think about making over ten thousand dollars in a month in just ninety days, you have to know what the proper mindset is in order to achieve that goal. You see, your mindset is extremely important to what you want to achieve. If you tell yourself you can't do something, then you won't be able to achieve it! So let's explore how you can have the proper money mindset in order to get rich!

First, let's take a look at an example of someone who has a money mindset and someone who doesn't. We'll take a look at two handymen. Handyman one, let's call him George, walks into a home and he is approached by the homeowner. The homeowner tells him or her they want crown molding put in their upstairs bathroom. George affably agrees it will make the appearance of their home nicer, but that's it.

Now, the second handyman's name is Josh. Josh walks into the home and he approaches the homeowner who tells him about wanting the crown molding. Josh also agrees it will look nicer, but he also goes on to explain how the crown molding will improve the value of the home over the long run.

Do you see the difference? George just wanted to make the home look better for aesthetic purpose only, but Josh saw the *value* in putting the crown molding in from an investment standpoint.

Being able to see the value in something is the money mindset. There are numerous other aspects to the money mindset, so let's take a look at them.

#1 **Mindful of the Long-Term**

There are many people out there who are looking to make money fast, but they rarely ever make a lot of it because of greed. Their first mindset is to think about what's in it for them. Rather, they should be thinking about how they can add as much value to someone else first. For example, it's like building credits with someone or an organization over the long-term. You might never need to use those credits, but if you do, help is returned in abundance. Don't allow your short-term greed destroy your long-term wealth.

#2 **You Deserve Only What You've Earned**

There is no room for an attitude of entitlement for someone when they have a money mindset. Don't expect to get to the corner office without paying your dues. At sixty-three years old, the man who put up the crown moldings is a great example of someone who doesn't expect something. He comes in with a good attitude to his job, does it well, cleans up, and leaves.

#3 You Believe You Deserve to be Wealthy

Money is out there for anyone to get their hands on. Once you believe you deserve to have that money, you'll subconsciously change your actions to make it happen. Stop feeling guilty about earning six figures in a year. There are people out there who earn seven and drive their companies into the ground to do it! Your mindset should not be 'why me' but 'why *not* me'? With the belief that you deserve to be wealthy too, your income will soar!

#4 You Ask Yourself What the Value of The Product or Service is Before You Spend a Dollar

People who have the money mindset are very value aware. Since they realize how hard it is to make money, they are much more careful about spending their money than the average person. They have to ask whether one dollar spent might return that dollar in the future. They are on the lookout for great deals and tend not to feel buyer's remorse because they purchase things that have a greater value than what they paid.

#5 You're Always Looking for Synergies and Leverage

When you go out to play tennis with people at a club or you're hanging out with some new friends, get excited! There could be synergies involved with those people. Not only are you having a good time with those people, but you are parlaying your relationship right into an excellent business opportunity. A website is an excellent example of leveraging assets to earn more. Besides earning advertising money, you can earn money by selling products and services. Your website can also serve as an online resume PR hub if you want to do more public works. If you haven't started a website, you really ought to!

#6 You Realize a Dollar Spent Today Could Grow To Much More In The Future

People who have the money mindset are naturally frugal. They despise letting go of too much money because they've already figured out what they spent today might have turned into if they had saved and invested at a ten percent rate of return over the following five to thirty years. Compound growth anchors money mindset people into spending less than they have earned. With an aggressive savings rate, you'll be surprised with just how much you could accumulate in a 401k in ten years.

#7 You're All About Tax Optimization

It's imperative to think about how much you have to earn before purchasing a particular item due to taxes. A car that costs $21,000 requires you to actually earn $30,000 in gross income. In terms of making money, someone who has a money mindset will look to reduce their taxes by figuring out the most tax friendly way they can make money passively, such as dividends. They also look to synergize their expenses if they are a freelancer or small business. There's no reason to do a company offsite in North Dakota if you can do one in Kauai. Figuring out how to pay little or no taxes becomes a hobby for someone with a money mindset.

#8 You Believe Excuses are No Excuse

You're either going to make it happen or you're going to fail. Failure is just fine; just don't make excuses and not do something about it. Figure out the reasons why you failed and then try again until you succeed. You need to believe you deserve only what you've earned, you take ownership for your failures and you most past them. Excuses are for those who blame the world for their shortcomings rather than themselves. The more excuses you use, the less you believe you are able to make things happen on your own.

#9 You Never Fail Due to a Lack of Effort

You can fail because your competition is incredibly talented, there was bad timing, or a natural disaster happened, but you will never fail due to a lack of doing your best. There are many people out there who say they are going to make a living writing or freelance programming, but most of them won't even send a draft of what they're writing to someone else for feedback. They don't want to put in the time to make the money.

#10 You Execute Solutions

Recognizing a problem or coming up with an idea is one thing. Coming up with the solution is more important. There are so many people out there who like to point out injustices or complain about something, but none of them doing anything about the situation. Someone with the money mindset will find a way to get it done and make it better.

If you read through this chapter and you believe you don't have the money mindset, don't despair! Anyone can develop the money mindset. The first step is to know you're worth it and believing that you deserve to be wealthy. If you put in the effort, there is no reason you can't be enjoying that passive income flow, too.

Now that you know what the money mindset is and you know where you have to change in order to become wealthy with passive income let's look at the amazing ways you can make ten thousand dollars in a month in just ninety days!

Chapter Two – Making Money as a Coach

Are you currently struggling to make money with your coaching business but you have an expectation to make ten thousand dollars a month? Stop struggling! It's absolutely possible to make six figures a year coaching business, and it can happen pretty fast if you follow the necessary steps you need in order to fill your e-mail list and focus on getting more calls.

These are the top tips for making ten thousand dollars a month or more in as little as ninety days. That doesn't mean it's going to happen overnight easily. Building a business takes some focus and some effort. The goal is to build relationships and help the ideal client solve specific problems they're facing, and you're the coach and mentor that can help them with the problem.

The first step is developing that money mindset. Having the right mindset is extremely important when it comes to almost anything in your life. Making a consistent ten thousand dollars a month is not an exception.

You can create a vision board in order to visualize your goal. Just cut out some pictures and words from a favorite magazine and add them to a pinboard. You can also create an online one with Pinterest that's private and filled with inspiring images and quotes!

Once you've developed the mindset, you need to test those coaching packages.

Test the Packages

Market research is the core principle of making a thriving coaching package and coaching business. Don't make a package you believe will sell. Create a package based off what your ideal client actually desires.

In the first module of testing your packages, you need to ask detailed questions of your target market to be sure you are going to make packages that will actually sell. Don't skip this step! Make your market research your priority.

If you already have packages that are not selling, then find out why. Ask the ideal client what they would like to see added to the package or if there is anything else you can help them with. Change your copywriting in order to put an emphasis on the benefits and allow the readers know exactly what they can expect to occur if they work with you.

Price the Packages

In order to bring your income goals to life, you need to price your services and packages accordingly. Many coaches undercharge for their services. But if you want to be someone who goes to exotic locations and has financial freedom, then you need to create a premium coaching package!

Perhaps the thought of charging more for your package frightens you. If this is the case, keep working on your money mindset and remind yourself that your services are worth it for your clients.

Making a good income from what you do for a living will help you not only have a happy, healthy life, but it will help you be of a greater service to your clients. You'll have more income you can invest in your education as a coach, which will help you keep enhancing your skills.

Here are the following action steps you should follow in this section:

1. Figure out how many of your current coaching packages you have to sell in order for you to make the ten thousand dollars a month.

2. Ask yourself if you are undercharging. If you are, increase your rates and make new packages.

3. Work on your money mindset and beliefs if you are bumping against statements like *I can't charge that much*. It's not your packages that are the problem, it's you.

Lead Generation

Ads are an excellent way to generate leads. In fact, they're so important when it comes to growing a coaching business that they are one of the essential keys to financial freedom! Try some Facebook or Google ads for your coaching business and you'll see it increase.

There are other ways you can generate leads, too, such as going through a guest post, doing a webinar, joint ventures, and teleclasses.

Whatever you choose to begin with, keeping going with it! Make sure to keep your efforts going so that your list grows with those are interested in getting to know you and the services you provide.

Here are the actions steps that will lead you to success!

1. Create some sort of lead generating strategy. How many leads to you require coming in so that you can hit ten thousand dollars a month? How many discovery or strategy sessions do you need to have to sign the number of clients you need in order to result in ten thousand dollars a month?

2. Invest time and learning in how to run Facebook ads or pay an expert to set them up for you.

3. Read and post on how to do a webinar.

4. Begin using Facebook ads or Google ads to promote your first webinar or opt-in gift.

Consistent Marketing

A successful coach will not flip-flop when it comes to their business. They will be consistent in marketing and expanding their reach. Ask yourself how consistent you are with marketing when it comes to your business. Are you in touch with your e-mail subscribers on a regular basis? What can your readers expect from a blog or newsletter? How do your readers feel about your brand and what are they learning from you?

Consistent marketing and lead generation helps you obtain more clients and hit your ten thousand dollar a month income. It's not rocket science. It's a formula that successful coaches and marketers have been following for some time.

Here are your action steps for continuous marketing.

1. Consider hiring a virtual assistant or hiring and intern for a few hours a week so you can focus on client generation activities.

2. Focus on some money making activities, such as getting leads, booking discovery calls, marketing, and much more. E-mail your list of contacts three times a week with one newsletter and two solo e-mails. Solo e-mails are the ones you send out that have a single call to action. It usually has something to do with income generation.

<u>Check out more books by Mark Thomas</u>

Thank you again for downloading this book!

If you enjoyed this book, then I'd like to ask you for a favor, would you be kind enough to leave a review for this book on Amazon? It'd be greatly appreciated!

Thank you and good luck! ☺

-Mark Thomas

www.ingramcontent.com/pod-product-compliance
Lightning Source LLC
Chambersburg PA
CBHW051729170526
45167CB00002B/855